EASY
SERVICE PROJECTS
FOR KIDS

SOCKS
FOR THE
HOMELESS

SHAY SPIVEY, BSW MSW

EASY SERVICE PROJECTS FOR KIDS:

SOCKS FOR THE HOMELESS

BY

SHAY SPIVEY, BSW, MSW

TABLE OF CONTENTS

CHAPTER ONE

Introduction

Hello, my name is Shay, and I've been collecting socks for the homeless for close to ten years.

Years ago, as a social work student, I was looking for an easy community service project. After serving at multiple homeless organizations, I learned a lot about their most challenging needs.

Every homeless shelter had desperate need for clean, new socks.

Socks are a recurring need, but most shelters rarely receive sock donations. I wanted to become a solution for that need.

I began with my family. For the holidays, I asked for packages of socks in place of gifts. Soon I was able to collaborate with my children's school to create a school-wide sock collection project. The first year we decorated a large box with wrapping paper, ribbons, and a sign asking for socks and placed it in the hallway near the front office. I created a flyer and the school gave permission to distribute it to the parents. We received over 120 pairs of socks and delivered them to a local homeless shelter.

The school was so excited by the results that we were allowed to host another socks drive the next year. This time I encouraged my oldest daughter come up with a new and exciting way to get the students involved. She came up the idea to create a classroom competition. Each classroom decorated a box and requested socks from staff, family, and friends. The classroom that collected the most socks was recognized by the school and given a party. It was a blast!

The sock drives were very successful and brought the students, staff, and families together for an excellent cause. Not only did we support a great cause, but my children gained leadership and project management skills along the way.

Over the years our non-profit organization, Socks For The Homeless, Inc., has coordinated multiple sock drives and partnered with schools, organizations, and businesses.

CHAPTER TWO

Why socks are important?

First, our mission is to help the homeless by providing socks through direct donations to homeless service organizations.

Second, we would like to raise awareness about the need for socks in the homeless community.

Third, we hope to encourage more people to create and coordinate service projects that serve the homeless in their communities.

#1

Homelessness

Homelessness is a serious problem everywhere!

There are many different reasons that individuals and families may experience homelessness such as poverty, job loss, domestic violence, incarceration, health issues, mental health challenges, substance abuse, loss of housing, etc.

#2

Needs

People experiencing homelessness face many challenges and have many needs, including but limited to lack of housing, unemployment, hunger, lack of access to healthcare, legal problems, mental health challenges, substance abuse, and education needs.

For example, on a single night in January 2015, 564,708 people were sleeping outside or in an emergency shelter or transitional housing program.

To learn more about these statitics, please check out the National Alliance to End Homelessness - State of Homeless Report at:

www.endhomelessness.org

#3

Sock donations needed

There is a constant, daily, regular need for clean, dry socks by the homeless community.

As an illustration, there are over one hundred homeless service organizations in the city of Indianapolis, Indiana.

Those organizations need sock donations regularly. Unfortunately, socks are one of the last contributions that people think to give, and the agencies run out frequently.

#4

Clean, dry, socks are important

Clean, dry socks offer essential protection for everyone's feet, especially in extreme weather.

For example, they protect your feet from frostbite and provide critical warmth in cold weather. In addition, socks provide padding, decrease friction, and absorb bacteria causing moisture in warmer weather.

#5

Mobile Population

The homeless spend most of their time walking from place to place. This constant mobility causes constant wear and tear on their feet, socks, and shoes. When your feet undergo significant stress throughout the day, a good pair of the socks will make a difference to prevent foot injuries and infections.

Because the homeless population is so mobile, their feet are put through a significant amount of stress throughout the day. A good pair of socks can go a long way in preventing foot problems.

Poor hygiene, limited access to showers, and other washing facilities can lead to infections and poor health. Wearing the clean, dry socks can go a long way towards good foot health.

#6

Recurring Need

The need for socks is a "recurrent need." This means that there is a constant, daily, regular need for clean, dry socks by the homeless community.

With limited access to washing facilities, the homeless can wear a single pair of socks for long periods of time or not at all. Worn out socks become thin, frayed, tattered, and a health hazard.

#7

Most needed item in shelters

The homeless put their socks through more wear and tear in a week than most socks see in a year.

Most are forced to sleep with their shoes on to prevent them from being stolen, and they spend most of their days walking. Foot wellness is a significant concern for overall physical wellbeing.

Homeless service organizations always need socks! Every day. Every month. Every year.

With limited to no income, damaged socks are hard to replace by individuals suffering from homelessness. So they often rely on the kindness of donated items.

Unfortunately, socks are often an overlooked clothing donation. But that's where you come in!

#8

Foot Health

Proper foot care is critical.

According to the Mayo Clinic, in cold conditions, frostbite may happen in thirty minutes or less.

Extreme weather, foot injuries, and infections can be harsh on the feet of homeless individuals, and in some cases deadly.

Health conditions like diabetes, which is prevalent in the homeless population, can further complicate the danger of inadequate foot care. Well-fitting and warm socks can be just as important as medication for diabetics to prevent skin ulcers, infections, and even tissue death.

CHAPTER THREE

Organizations

Most people in the homeless community are not able to buy new socks regularly. So, to fill this need organizations give new socks to people in need for free.

Donations to homeless service organizations often come from schools, church groups, service clubs, colleges and other concerned citizens.

Following is a list of programs that specialize in collecting socks for the homeless.

1.
BOMBAS

Website:

www.bombas.com

Program Description:

Bombas is an athletic-leisure sock company that partners with organizations to distribute socks to those in need. They donate all over the United States to charity organizations.

2.

SOCKS FOR THE HOMELESS, INC.

Indianapolis, Indiana

Email: shayspivey@yahoo.com

Website:

socksforthehomeless.blogspot.com

Program Description:

Socks for the Homeless, Inc. is a community service project the collects socks and donates to homeless service organizations in the Indianapolis area. They partner with organizations, businesses, and schools to coordinate sock drives.

3.

THE JOY OF SOX

580 Lindsey Dr., Suite 150

Radnor, PA 19087-2339 USA

Office Phone: 610-688-3318 office

Fax: 610-788-2133

Website:

www.thejoyofsox.org

Program Description:

The mission of *The Joy of Sox* is simply to provide joy to the homeless with new socks. They offer new socks for the homeless all across the United States.

4.

COMFORT SOCKS FOR THE HOMELESS

PO Box 477

Supply, NC 28462

Phone: 910.269.8577

Website:

www.comfortsocks.org

Program Description:

Comfort Socks is a public charity that gives new socks to homeless shelters and non-profits who primarily serve the homeless population all across the United States.

5.

SOCKS AND CHOCS

England

Website:

www.socksandchocs.co.uk

Program Description:

Socks and Chocs delivers socks, chocolates, and other needed items to homeless shelters in the British cities of Coventry, Birmingham, Wolverhampton and Worcester (England).

6.

JUST SOCKS FOUNDATION, INC.

388 Bloor Street East, Suite 1203

Toronto ON, M4W 3W9

Phone: 416-993-1718

Email: info@justsocks.ca

Website:

www.justsocks.ca

Program Description:

Just Socks provides new socks to the homeless of Canada. They raise funds for new sock donations to give to registered Canadian charities serving the homeless and less fortunate in Canada.

7.

HOPE MISSION'S SUMMER SOCK DRIVE

Website:

www.hopemission.com/general-news/hope-missions-summer-sock-drive/

Program Description:

Their mission is to donate thousands of clothing items, including socks to the homeless men and women in Edmonton. You can bring socks to Hope Mission Center for your contribution.

8.

SOCKTOBER

Website:

www.soulpancake.com/socktober/

Program Description:

They are working to provide socks to homeless and needy people all over America. They give socks to homeless shelters and organizations.

9.

YOUR CITY SPORTS

Canada and the USA

Website:

www.yourcitysports.com

Program Description:

They sell high-quality athletic socks and donate a new pair for homeless charity for each sold pair. They are giving socks to charities in Canada and the USA.

10.

KNOCK, KNOCK, GIVE A SOCK

Website:

www.knockknockgiveasock.org/where-we-donate.html

Program Description:

They provide socks for homeless people, and they denote socks in Binghamton, New York City, Philadelphia, PA and New Jersey, Los Angeles and Philadelphia, PA.

EASY SERVICE PROJECTS FOR KIDS: SOCKS FOR THE HOMELESS

11.

RUBY A. NEESON DIABETES AWARENESS FOUNDATION, INC.

Atlanta, GA

Website:

http://www.fightdiabetesnow.org/Sock-Drive.html

Program Description:

Ruby A. Neeson Diabetes Foundation is a community, and they collect new socks to distribute in the metropolitan Atlanta. Foot care is essential for diabetics, and homeless people face difficulties in the treatment of lots of health problems.

EASY SERVICE PROJECTS FOR KIDS: SOCKS FOR THE HOMELESS

12.
TEEN FEED

Website:

www.teenfeed.org/blog/donate/winter-sock-basic-needs-drives-for-youth/

Program Description:

Teen Feed works to provide basic items and daily essentials to needy people. You can help them by giving socks and other essential items. They drop their donations on Tuesdays and Thursdays at University Congregation Church.

13.

SOCKS IN THE CITY

8 Cambridge Street

West Leederville, Western Australia, 6007

Website:

www.socksinthecity.com.au

Program Description:

Socks In The City offers free socks to homeless in Australia.

14.

HANES

Website:

www.hanes.com/hanesforgood

Program Description:

Hanes donates almost 200,000 pairs of socks to homeless people across the United States.

15.

NIGHT WATCH

21181

Seattle, WA 98111

Phone: 206-323-4359

Website:

www.seattlenightwatch.org/sockit.htm

Program Description:

Night Watch conducts a drive called "Sock it to Homelessness." They accept new and old pairs of socks.

16.

HANNAH'S SOCKS

Website:

www.hannahssocks.org

Program Description:

Hannah's Socks provides socks for homeless people to keep their feet warm and avoid health problems. It's a non-profit organization and working in Perrysburg, OH 43551.

17.

SOCK IT TO EM

Colorado

Website:

www.sockittoemsockcampaign.org

Program Description:

Sock It To Em provides socks to homeless in December, and you can drop socks at Susan Elizabeth Lee Ridge Plaza Dr. Castle Rock CO 80108.

18.

ORIGINAL JOLLIE GOODS

England

Website:

www.jolliegoods.com/giving

Program Description:

To keep the feet of homeless, poor and needy people, they offer socks to many homeless charities and their clients. They are registered in England to provide socks to homeless people.

CHAPTER FOUR

Let's Get Involved

Homeless shelters can't do this without you!
They need partners like you in the community to
replenish their sock supply on a regular basis.

As individuals, we can have a small impact, but together
in collaboration with other organizations, we can
impact thousands of lives over and over again.

Let's work together to provide this small, often
forgotten, clothing article to help provide warmth and
comfort to our most vulnerable neighbors!

.

"By organizing a sock drive at your office, school, place of worship, or even with friends and family, you not only help keep our community's homeless healthy and safe, but you also help people maintain their dignity and comfort during a difficult time in their lives."

Friends of Boston's Homeless, 2016

www.fobh.org

CHAPTER FIVE

Sock collection project ideas

Business

Are you looking for a fun holiday project? Sock drives are great for team building activities and company community service projects.

Ideas:
- Employee socks drive
- Become a sock drop location for the community.

Organizations
(Sororities, fraternities, community, etc....)

Sock drives are great for community service projects and volunteer hours.

Ideas:

- Make it a competition and encourage members and friends to ask for donations.
- Host an event or party to collect sock donations.
- Bring awareness to the community.

Schools

Students, staff, parents, and the community can be involved in this type of school wide service project. Sock collections are great for community service hours, volunteer opportunities, and academic resumes.

Ideas:
- Plan a school sock drive
- Create a classroom competition
- Become a sock drop location for the community.
- Educate students about the need

Churches

Sock collection projects are a great way to give back to the community.

Ideas:

- Create a festive sock drive for Sunday school classes.
- Get creative and make it a large event
- Become a sock drop location for the community.
- Host a community sock drive

Individuals

Sock collection projects are a great way to help others.

Ideas:

- Create a sock drive at work, with family, in the neighborhood, at church, etc.
- Great for community service projects and volunteer hours.
- Get creative and host a neighborhood sock drive.

OTHER EASY SERVICE PROJECT IDEAS FOR KIDS

Make holiday cards for senior citizens.

***

Collect blankets and toiletries for the homeless.

***

Bake cookies for a homeless shelter.

***

Host a book drive for a children's hospital.

***

Decorate placemats for "Meals on Wheels."

***

Donate blankets to "Project Linus"

***

Organize a neighborhood food drive.

***

Volunteer to read for children at the library.

***

Donate baby and children's clothes to a women's shelter.

***

Collect school supplies for homeless children.

***

Put on gloves and pick up trash at your local park.

***

Coordinate a schoolwide competition to collect clothing for refugees.

***

Volunteer at your local animal shelter.

***

Send a thank you letter to a service member.

***

Donate books and school supplies to donate to girls' education organizations in developing countries. Learn more at:

Educate Girls Around The World

***

Raise money for a local animal shelter.

***

Start a garden and donate food to a food bank.

***

Collect used towels to donate to your local animal shelter.

***

Plant a tree.

***

Create a lemonade stand and donate the profits to a service organization of your choice.

***

Collect gently used children's shoes to donate to a children's emergency shelter.

***

Create care packages for a nursing home or children's hospital.

***

OTHER BOOKS BY SHAY SPIVEY

Educate Girls Around the World: Good People Doing Good Work

FREE Money for Education Series:

How to Submit a Winning Scholarship Application: Secret Techniques I Used to Win $100,000 in College Scholarships

How to Find Scholarships and Free Financial Aid for Private High Schools

Where to Find FREE Money for College

FREE Tuition Colleges 2016

Find FREE Money for Graduate School

FREE Tuition Colleges for Adults 50+

Understanding Scholarships and Financial Aid

Comprensión De Becas Y Ayuda Financiera

Prepare for College Series:

REFERENCES

www.endhomelessness.org

www.thejoyofsox.org/ten-facts-about-socks-feet-and-homelessness/

www.comfortsocks.org/pdfs/The_Importance_of_Socks.pdf

www.pointsoflight.org/blog/2014/06/04/when-socks-are-more-important-food%E2%80%99

www.mc.vanderbilt.edu:8080/reporter/index.html?ID=8552

www.farmingtonvoice.com/hills-bank-hosts-sock-it-to-me-drive-121900

Friends of Boston's Homeless (2016).
www.fobh.org

www.ingramcontent.com/pod-product-compliance
Lightning Source LLC
Chambersburg PA
CBHW051325220526
45468CB00004B/1498